PLOT *a* COURSE

The Workbook

Plot-A-Course: The Workbook, by Marchesa Schroeder

Published by Marchesa Schroeder

Copyright © 2020 by Marchesa Schroeder

All rights reserved. No portion of this book may be reproduced in any form without permission from the publisher, except as permitted by U.S. copyright law.

Cover design, interior design, typography/typesetting, editing, graphics, and artwork by Marchesa Schroeder

Paperback book ISBN: 978-1-7342683-4-8

For bulk ordering inquiries contact:
Plotacoursecontact@gmail.com

TABLE OF *contents*

1   **Carrots & Confetti**

2   **Vow of Commitment**

4   **Exercise 1:** Good Memories = Good Feelings

10   **Brainstorming**

11   **Exercise 2:** Best Possible Self

13   **Make Choices**

14   **Exercise 3:** Experience Personal Excellence

16   **Exercise 4:** Positive Cognition Affirmations

18   **Long & Short-Term Goals**

19   **Exercise 6:** My Current Life Situation

22	**Quadrant Theory of Focus**
25	**Commitments & Obligations**
27	**Identifying & Setting Personal Boundaries**
29	**Actionable Steps**
31	**Health Goals**
32	**Business Goals**
33	**Financial Goals**
34	**Relationship Goals**
35	**Self-Trust**
36	**Daily List**
37	**Supplies List**
38	**Contacts**
40	**Monthly Budget**

This PAC Workbook belongs to:

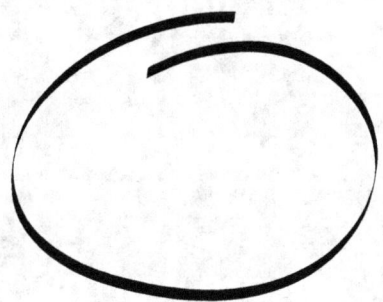

Everything is okay.

Life is good, things are interesting and people love you.

You are on the right path.

You are worthy.

I believe in you.

Carrots & Confetti

What Carrots & Confetti might you use to reward yourself after each milestone?

CARROTS

_____

_____

_____

_____

_____

_____

_____

_____

CONFETTI

_____

_____

_____

_____

_____

_____

_____

_____

The Vow of Commitment to Yourself

Today, I take a vow of commitment to myself. In this vow, I agree to commit fully to myself and to my unique journey. I vow to love, cherish, trust, and care for all parts of myself, always, in all ways. I vow to comfort, support and embrace myself in times of less than optimal emotional and physical health. I vow to apply the PAC principles that I find meaningful and appropriate to my life, knowing that it's in my own personal best interest to do so. I embrace the ultimate truth that my goal is to feel good. I vow to allow myself the ability to experience good feelings as often as genuinely possible. I promise to love and respect all versions of myself, always in all ways. I promise to be my own best friend, acting in a way that is kind while offering support, understanding, and motivation to myself. I promise to challenge myself to be my best self, being aware and accepting of boundaries when they become apparent. I vow to treat others as I would like to be treated: with respect, care, understanding, compassion, honesty, and love. I vow to treat all forms of life with respect, understanding that we all contribute to this spectacular experience of life. I entrust myself with the responsibility of my own life, knowing I have my best interest at heart. I accept responsibility for my own happiness, the frequency of my good feelings, and the quality of my life. I vow to celebrate the honest and diligent efforts I put forth. I vow to release attachment the outcomes. I believe I have the power, faith, love, and ability to enjoy my life. I vow to love the life I lead. I vow to be unapologetically, lovingly, authentically me. Today, I commit to myself.

---

signature & date:

COMMITMENT REFLECTION

Why does this commitment matter to you?

_____

_____

_____

_____

_____

Why have you chosen to make this commitment now?

_____

_____

_____

_____

_____

How do you believe following through with this commitment will impact your life for the better? In what specific ways? How might this decision impact those around you in a positive way?

_____

_____

_____

_____

Who have you chosen to share your commitment with? Why?

_____

_____

_____

_____

Exercise 1
Good Memories = Good Feelings

To get started, answer the following questions in vivid detail.

What is one of your favorite memories?
(Who were you with, where were you, and what were you doing? How did you feel in the moment? Who was there? What was the weather like? Can you describe the environment?)

_____
_____
_____
_____
_____
_____
_____
_____
_____
_____

What was one of the happiest moments of your life?

_____

_____

_____

_____

_____

_____

_____

_____

_____

When did you feel the most accomplished?
Was it when you had your first child? When you fell in love? Graduated school? When your mother congratulated you for going to the bathroom for the first time on your own?

_____

_____

_____

_____

_____

_____

_____

_____

_____

_____

_____

_____

_____

Who are you most grateful for in this moment? Why?

_____

_____

_____

_____

_____

_____

_____

_____

_____

_____

_____

_____

_____

_____

What brought the most joy in your life?

_____

_____

_____

_____

_____

_____

_____

_____

_____

_____

_____

_____

_____

_____

_____

Level up Opportunity

Another great way to explore good memories is by going through an old photo album, book, box, or diary! If you feel inspired, take the next 15 minutes (set a timer) to explore something that reminds you of a good time in your past, such as flipping through a photo album. Once you start to remember those times, explore them in depth, asking who you were with, what you were doing, how you felt, and any other detailed descriptions that come to mind.

Brainstorming Tips:

- Allow Yourself Ample Time
- Accept That No Goals Are Too Great, Too Small, or "Unrealistic"
- Take Breaks

In the space provided on the next page, write down everything and anything you want to do and have done. This is a brainstorming exercise so rid yourself of inhibitions and write down whatever comes to your mind in this moment, knowing that this list will likely change in the future! *Remember: nothing is too small or too big to write down. Don't worry about phrasing and don't worry about keeping things "realistic". Just let it all out!

Goal determination is the fun part. From my experience, this is the exercise that generates excitement and energy flow. The only rule in this practice is to free yourself from rules and confines. If you can dream it, you can do it. The goal for your "goals list" is to write down everything that comes to mind that you desire. If you want to be the president of the United States, the next Drake, number 1 on the Forbes list of Most Eligible Bachelors, own your own coffee shop, have a 6-pack, be a model—the possibilities are endless! **Write it all down.** The idea is to expand the list as wide and extensive as you'd like and then you can retract, prioritize, and filter later.

Some of the most common goal attainment areas include: Physical Health, Personal, Social, Work/Career, Family, Financial, Mind/Intellect, Spirituality. So feel free to include these. Remember: Goals can be (and often are) feelings, so I encourage you to write those down as well! (ie: Your goal is to feel happy often, to feel love, to give love, to feel patient, etc.)

Brainstorming

Exercise 2
Best Possible Self

What is the best possible future you can imagine?
What are you doing with your time? Who are you with? Where are you? How do you feel? What is the weather like? How did you get to where you are at? Imagine the most optimal future in regard to each major area of your life: career, relationships, hobbies, academia, and health (personal & environmental).

_____

_____

_____

_____

_____

_____

_____

_____

_____

BRAINSTORM GOALS & DREAMS REFLECTION

After having completed this exercise, how are you feeling?
_____
_____
_____
_____
_____

Did anything come up for you emotionally during this exercise?
_____
_____
_____
_____
_____

If time and resources were of no concern, where would you go and what would you do? Would you be by yourself or with others? I encourage you to be specific about the details and, of course, your feelings!
_____
_____
_____
_____

Level up opportunity! Repeat this exercise every day for 15 days (20 minutes a day) and record your observations below.
(Remember: Your thoughts inspire your actions!)
_____
_____
_____
_____

Make Choices

*"You will always have the exactly equal opportunity
to enjoy yourself regardless of the choice."*

GOALS TO FOCUS ON   TIMELINE FOR COMPLETION

*As long as you feel good, being guided by your moral
compass and values, no one choice is better than another.*

Exercise 3
Experience Personal Excellence

This is a simple exercise focused on personal excellence: that is, trying your very best and quantifying what that means by a measurement of your own standards and abilities. In this exercise, you will set out to do your best at one hyper specific thing. This could be dribbling a basketball, singing one note or a line in a song, writing a stellar paragraph. Choose to try your best at anything you find value in. For that one moment, that one thing, give it your undivided attention and complete energy. Do it to the very best of your current ability. Then, answer the questions below.

How might you incorporate personal excellence into your life from this point forward?

_____
_____
_____
_____
_____

What did you choose to do your best at and why?

_____
_____
_____
_____
_____

PERSONAL EXCELLENCE REFLECTION

After having completed this exercise, how are you feeling?

_____
_____
_____
_____
_____

Is there another time that you can remember when you experienced personal excellence? If so, when?

_____
_____
_____
_____
_____

Did any other emotions or thoughts come up before or after the exercise?

_____
_____
_____
_____

"

__The cost of our goals is the life we exchange in pursuit of them__ and because the outcome of your attempts can never be guaranteed, you owe it to yourself to enjoy the pursuit itself. Enjoy the pursuit knowing you gain knowledge and experience from every single path you walk down.

Exercise 4
Positive Cognition Affirmations

The Positive Cognitive Affirmations exercise is a Plot-A-Course original, founded on the concept that what we place our focus on will grow. The goal for this exercise is to strengthen your positive beliefs by providing evidence that supports them.

List 3 of your positive cognitions (beliefs) and provide 3 examples of supporting evidence.

1. _____
   (belief)

   → _____
   (support)

   → _____
   (support)

   → _____
   (support)

2. _____
   (belief)

   → _____
      (support)

   → _____
      (support)

   → _____
      (support)

3. _____
   (belief)

   → _____
      (support)

   → _____
      (support)

   → _____
      (support)

Long & Short-Term Goals

*Categorize each of your previously identified goals (from the Brainstorming/Making Choices sections) into either long-term or short-term goals. *Remember, some goals will fall on both lists**

LONG-TERM GOALS

_____

_____

_____

_____

_____

_____

_____

_____

_____

SHORT-TERM GOALS

_____

_____

_____

_____

_____

_____

_____

_____

_____

Exercise 6
My Current Life Situation

In the space below, list all of the factors you can think of that contribute to your life situation. Remember, you are an alien who is trying to piece together, without judgment or emotion, who you are, where you are, and what you have. To get started, ask yourself the following questions: *What kind of car am I driving? How much money do I have in the bank? What kinds of debt loads do I have? How do I spend my time? Who do I spend my time with? What types of food do I eat? What types of relationships do I have? How often do I exercise?*

MY CURRENT LIFE SITUATION

MY CURRENT LIFE SITUATION

IDENTIFY YOUR LIFE SITUATION, BRO
REFLECTION

What privileges, resources, and opportunities are available to you right now? How might they help you on your path towards attaining your goals?

_____
_____
_____
_____
_____
_____
_____
_____

Describe a time in the past you overcame an obstacle or challenge. How did it feel?

_____
_____
_____
_____
_____
_____
_____
_____

• • • • • • • • • • • • • • • • • • • •

Obstacles are opportunities in disguise.

• • • • • • • • • • • • • • • • • • • •

The PAC
Quadrant Theory of Focus

HIGH STRESS ZONE

Q1
Urgent!
&
Important!

COMFORTABLE

Q2
NOT Urgent
&
Important!

Q3
Urgent!
&
NOT Important

Q4
NOT Urgent
&
NOT Important

INTERRUPTIONS

DISTRACTIONS

In the quadrants below, list out all of the tasks, commitments, and obligations you have.

Remember: Someone else's emergency does not have to be yours.

Q1 = Urgent and Important
High Stress Zone

Q2 = Not Urgent and Important
Comfortable

Q3 = Urgent and Not Important
Interruptions

Q4 = Not Urgent and Not Important
Distractions

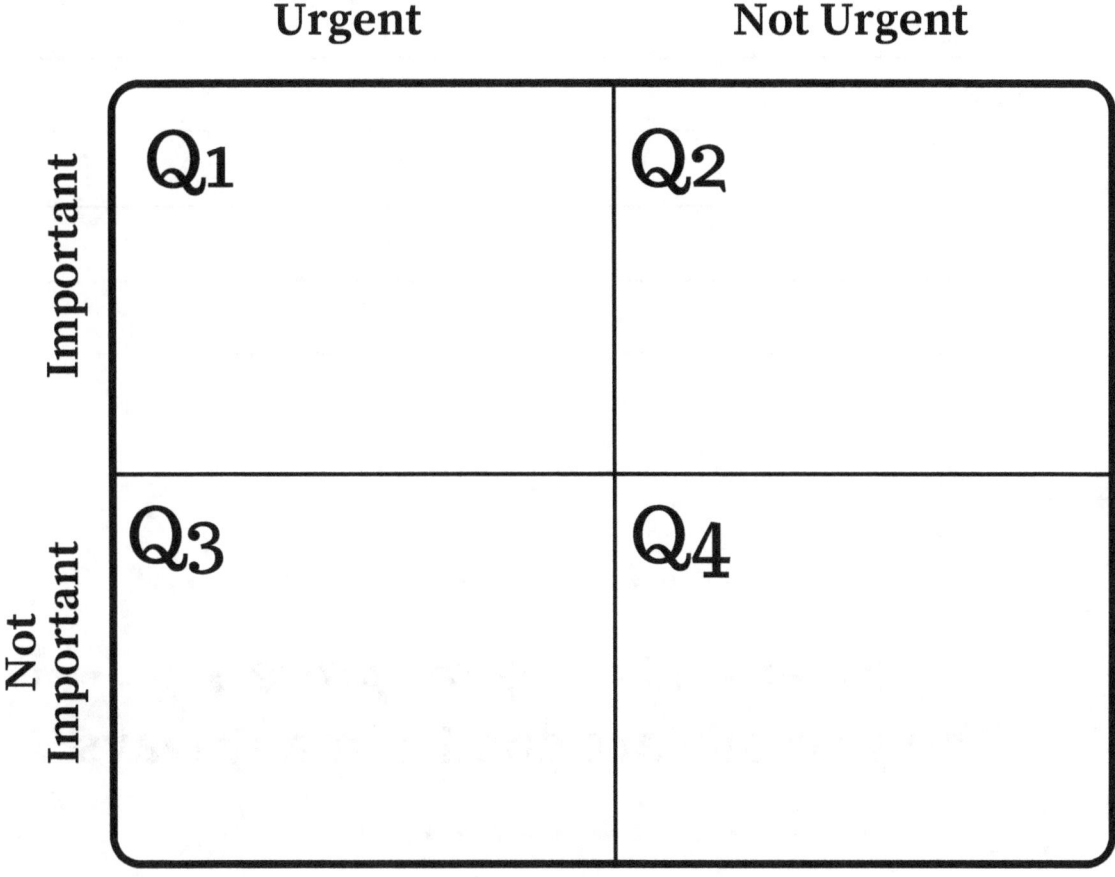

QUADRANT THEORY OF FOCUS REFLECTION

What important tasks can you address now (Q2) before they become urgent and important (Q1)?

_____
_____
_____
_____
_____
_____
_____

Are there any fillers or distractions (Q4) in your life that you would like to redirect your energy from?

_____
_____
_____
_____
_____
_____
_____

• •

**Relax and *enjoy the process*.
Things really are good in many ways.**

• •

Create a List of All Commitments & Obligations

COMMITMENTS & OBLIGATIONS

☐ _____ ☐ _____
☐ _____ ☐ _____
☐ _____ ☐ _____
☐ _____ ☐ _____
☐ _____ ☐ _____
☐ _____ ☐ _____
☐ _____ ☐ _____
☐ _____ ☐ _____
☐ _____ ☐ _____
☐ _____ ☐ _____

*Control what you can, accept what you can't,
and learn from your "mistakes."*

COMMITMENTS & OBLIGATIONS REFLECTION

What actions might you take now to prevent a commitment or obligation from reaching Quadrant 1?

_____

_____

_____

_____

_____

_____

Can any of your tasks or responsibilities be delegated to someone (or something) else?

_____

_____

_____

_____

_____

_____

What personal deadlines can you set for each of your responsibilities and obligations?

_____

_____

_____

_____

Celebrate the honest and diligent efforts you put forth. Then, embrace whatever the outcome may be.

Identifying & Setting Personal Boundaries

*Boundaries can include your **physical space** (your body and home), your **interpersonal relationships** (significant other, boss, coworker), and your **emotional/mental** sphere (beliefs and ideas).*

In the spaces below list out your personal boundaries, how they could be violated, and what you might do to enforce them in a healthy way.

PERSONAL BOUNDARY	HOW IT WAS/COULD BE VIOLATED	WHAT YOU CAN DO TO ENFORCE IT
ie: No phone calls between 7-8 am	People forget and call during those hours	Gently remind them not to call between those hours unless it's an emergency

PERSONAL BOUNDARY	HOW IT WAS/COULD BE VIOLATED	WHAT YOU CAN DO TO ENFORCE IT

Reflection:

- What are some potential consequences of enforcing a boundary in this way?

- How might you react if others enforced their boundaries in this way?

- How effective might this way be?

Actionable Steps

*Write out a list of actionable steps next to each one of your chosen goals. *Remember, your ultimate goal is **Good Feelings***

GOAL:

ACTIONABLE STEPS

- [ ] _____
- [ ] _____
- [ ] _____
- [ ] _____
- [ ] _____
- [ ] _____
- [ ] _____
- [ ] _____
- [ ] _____
- [ ] _____

GOAL:

ACTIONABLE STEPS

- [ ] _____
- [ ] _____
- [ ] _____
- [ ] _____
- [ ] _____
- [ ] _____
- [ ] _____
- [ ] _____
- [ ] _____
- [ ] _____

GOAL:

ACTIONABLE STEPS

- ☐ _____
- ☐ _____
- ☐ _____
- ☐ _____
- ☐ _____
- ☐ _____

GOAL:

ACTIONABLE STEPS

- ☐ _____
- ☐ _____
- ☐ _____
- ☐ _____
- ☐ _____
- ☐ _____

GOAL:

ACTIONABLE STEPS

- ☐ _____
- ☐ _____
- ☐ _____
- ☐ _____
- ☐ _____

GOAL:

ACTIONABLE STEPS

- ☐ _____
- ☐ _____
- ☐ _____
- ☐ _____
- ☐ _____

Health Goals

Physical, Mental, Emotional, Spiritual

Business/Career Goals

Non-financial

Financial Goals

Relationship Goals

Social/Family/Friends/Partner

Self-Trust

*"If you find that you can't trust yourself in this moment, that's perfectly okay. You just learned something that you can use to empower yourself. Accept it and let the good feelings flow by **growing to learn to trust yourself.**"*

PROMISES I AM MAKING TO MYSELF

- ☐ ie: Wake up at 4 a.m. tomorrow
- ☐
- ☐
- ☐
- ☐
- ☐
- ☐
- ☐
- ☐
- ☐

Reflection:

- Did you follow through with the promises you made to yourself? If so, how did it feel? If not, how might you adjust your personal promises to be more achievable?

- Have you noticed any running inner dialogue? Has it been helpful or unhelpful?

DAILY LIST

Date: _____

-
-
-
-
-
-
-

-
-
-
-
-
-
-

Notes:

Supplies List

Daily Supplies List

- ☐ _____
- ☐ _____
- ☐ _____
- ☐ _____
- ☐ _____
- ☐ _____
- ☐ _____
- ☐ _____
- ☐ _____
- ☐ _____
- ☐ _____
- ☐ _____
- ☐ _____
- ☐ _____

Future Supplies List

- ☐ _____
- ☐ _____
- ☐ _____
- ☐ _____
- ☐ _____
- ☐ _____
- ☐ _____
- ☐ _____
- ☐ _____
- ☐ _____
- ☐ _____
- ☐ _____
- ☐ _____
- ☐ _____

Contacts

Name

Address:

Email:

Phone:
 Notes:

Name

Address:

Email:

Phone:
 Notes:

Name

Address:

Email:

Phone:
 Notes:

Name

Address:

Email:

Phone:
 Notes:

Name		Name	
Address:		Address:	
Email:		Email:	
Phone:		Phone:	
Notes:		Notes:	

Name		Name	
Address:		Address:	
Email:		Email:	
Phone:		Phone:	
Notes:		Notes:	

Monthly Budget

Housing
- *Mortgage/Rent*
- *Electricity/Gas/Water*
- *Garbage/Recycle*
- *Maintenance/Repairs*
- *TV, Internet*
- *Phone*

Loans
- *Student/Credit cards*

Transportation
- *Car payment*
- *Gas*
- *Insurance/Registration*
- *Public Transit/Uber*

Nutrition
- *Groceries*
- *Dining out*
- *Vitamins/supplements*

Health
- *Insurance*
- *Beauty (nails, hair, etc)*

Entertainment
- *Movies*
- *Concert*

Miscellaneous

MONTH	INCOME	EXPENSES	TOTAL
JAN	+$	-$	$
FEB	+$	-$	$
MARCH	+$	-$	$
APRIL	+$	-$	$
MAY	+$	-$	$
JUNE	+$	-$	$
JULY	+$	-$	$
AUG	+$	-$	$
SEP	+$	-$	$
OCT	+$	-$	$
NOV	+$	-$	$
DEC	+$	-$	$

For merchandise, book releases, and all things PAC, head over to:

www.plotacourse.net

PAC Life Leader Stickers

Plot-A-Course Notepads

Plot-A-Course Bookmarks

Want to get inspiration, tips, tricks, and life hacks to lead a "good-feelings-centered" life?

Go to www.plotacourse.net/newsletter and sign up for the newsletter.

Welcome to the PAC Tribe!
www.instagram.com/plotacourse_book
www.plotacourse.net

www.ingramcontent.com/pod-product-compliance
Lightning Source LLC
Chambersburg PA
CBHW081128080526
44587CB00021B/3798